J599.2   AC 47957

Darling, Kathy

Tasmanian Devil

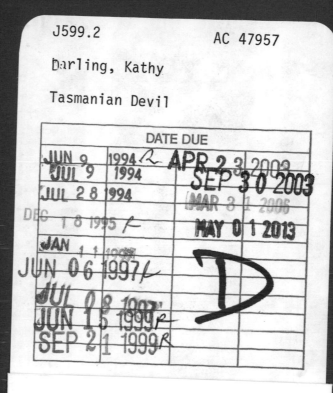

DATE DUE			
JUN 9 1994	APR 2 3 2003		
JUL 9 1994	SEP 3 0 2003		
JUL 2 8 1994	MAR 3 1 2006		
DEC 1 8 1995	MAY 0 1 2013		
JAN 1 1 1997			
JUN 0 6 1997			
JUL 0 8 1997	D		
JUN 1 5 1999			
SEP 2 1 1999			

Tasmanian Devil

Tasmanian Devil

ON LOCATION

KATHY DARLING

PHOTOGRAPHS BY TARA DARLING

LOTHROP, LEE & SHEPARD BOOKS   NEW YORK

ACKNOWLEDGMENTS

Dr. John Kirsch, Director of the University of Wisconsin Zoological Museum. Thank you for sharing your firsthand knowledge of devils and for checking the manuscript for accuracy.

Tasmanian Devil Park, Port Arthur, Tasmania. Thanks to John and Caroline Hamilton for allowing us to photograph the baby devils born at their marvelous zoo.

Warner Bros. Inc. for permission to use the cartoon character Tasmanian Devil (Taz™), who has given us so much pleasure.

Australian scientists Michael Archer and Eric Guiler, whose field work and writing provided much background information.

Lindsay Smith of the Australian Overseas Information Service and Kevin Arnold of the Tasmanian Tourist Board, for helping us find the research site and for showing us what real Aussie hospitality is.

Cradle Mountain Lodge, Tasmania. The P&O Resort is a perfect place for devil watching. The lodge owners and all those who work there really care about the welfare of the guests and, even more important, about the wildlife that surrounds this special hotel. Special thanks to Cary Scotton. Also to the cooks who kept us supplied with devil bait!

Library of Congress Cataloging in Publication Data   Darling, Kathy.   Tasmanian devil : on location / Kathy Darling ; photographs by Tara Darling.   p.   cm. — (On location)   Summary: Describes the physical characteristics, behavior, and eating habits of the Tasmanian devil.   ISBN 0-688-09726-X. — ISBN 0-688-09727-8 (lib. bdg.)   1. Tasmanian devil—Pictorial works—Juvenile literature.   I. Darling, Tara.   II. Title.   QL737.M33D37   1992   599.2—dc20   91-27561   CIP   AC

Contents

The Tasmanian devil is a super sniffer. Its nose is almost a hundred times more sensitive than that of a human.

Night on Devil Mountain

December 24—
Cradle Mountain National Park
Tasmania, Australia

A small animal, black as the night around him, stood in the middle of a rain-forest trail. He lifted his nose and sniffed the breeze. *Meat.* The scent in the air was rotten meat. Glorious rotten meat! He began to move down the trail, occasionally breaking into a clumsy, rolling gallop in his eagerness to reach his favorite food. When his sensitive nose told him other animals were moving toward *his* meat, he screamed in rage.

The tempting smell was that of a dead turkey that Tara and I had wired to a tree on Christmas Eve. Huddling behind a rock in the cold, dark rain forest, watching a bait tree and waiting for a devil, was a strange way to spend the holiday.

When we heard the horrible, blood-curdling scream, we knew a devil was near. We had waited for hours to see a Tasmanian devil; but now that one was near, we didn't know whether to be excited or afraid. If the devil was trying to scare us, it was doing a mighty good job.

At the edge of the clearing we saw an animal standing quietly in the shadows. He was about the size of a house cat. Surprisingly cautious, the animal sniffed the

The devil doesn't know this meat is held by wires.

breeze and circled all around the clearing. He kept to the cover of the bushes and avoided open places. It was a few minutes before he felt confident enough to make a try for the bait. Surely this shy little animal was not the dreaded Tasmanian devil we had come on location to find.

The animal grabbed the meat. He tried to pull the turkey into the bushes, but the heavy wires stopped him. The little black and white animal shook the turkey and screamed in obvious rage. There was no doubt in our minds now. This was a Tasmanian devil.

He was a very angry devil. And a hungry one too, judging from the way he kept tugging and pulling at the turkey. The wires held the meat securely even when he shook it. It took that devil five minutes to figure out that the turkey was tied to the tree. But the moment he located the thick wires, he cut them with a single bite

But when he discovers the wire, cutting it is no problem for teeth that were designed to crush bones.

and dragged the turkey, which weighed as much as he did, into the bushes.

We had just witnessed the awesome power of the Tasmanian devil. If any land animal deserves to be nicknamed "Jaws," this night hunter does. Devils have the most powerful bite of any animal their size. In fact, some biologists believe that only two animals have stronger jaws—the great white shark and the hyena.

The Christmas visitor, which we named Side Spot for the white dot on his side, had made off with our best bait. We didn't want it to happen again, so we anchored the meat we had left with twice as many wires. Another young devil, one with white chest markings, came and chomped through the wires as easily as Side Spot had.

Now all we had for bait were some leftovers from lunch and the turkey guts, which we scattered around the clearing.

Imagine how surprised we were to see

Cradle Mountain National Park. The shaggy-haired kangaroo in the button grass meadow is a Bennett's wallaby. It is one of the devils' favorite foods.

Side Spot back for a second helping. He had dragged off an entire turkey and here he was, a few hours later, cramming lengths of intestine into his mouth like bloody spaghetti. While he was eating, another devil screamed from the rain forest, and Side Spot, with the guts hanging out of his mouth, screamed back. He looked nervous as he peered all around him, and then began to eat faster. When the challenger raced out of the bushes and tried to get some of the food, Side Spot chased him off. Other night creatures, attracted by the smell of our bait, came into the clearing: possums, catlike quolls, and the tiny kangaroos called pademelons (PAD-ee-mel-unz). Side Spot made sure they didn't stay long.

Cradle Mountain National Park, the location of our devil watch, stretches 50 miles across the central highlands of Tasmania, a heart-shaped island 120 miles off the south coast of Australia. Here devils roam through *cool* rain forest. Giant gum trees, the tallest flowering plants in the world, form canopies 300 feet high, and mounds of button grass dot meadows that are covered with snow for more than six months a year. By day, the devils sleep. But at night, their eerie cries, unchallenged by any other animal's, echo like thunder in the jagged hills. The devil is king of these mountains.

Because they are nocturnal and solitary and many people find them repulsive, devils have not been well studied. Much about their life history is not known. There are many great discoveries waiting for any young scientists who are not afraid to follow the devil's path.

What the Devil Is a Devil?

Ugly. Dangerous. Scary. Smelly. Mangy. Bloodthirsty. These and most of the other words used to describe Tasmanian devils are not complimentary. They are one of the most hated and feared animals in the world.

In the early days of Tasmanian settlement, devils were thought to be savage livestock killers, and bounties were paid for their destruction. Terrifying stories have been told about how devils chase and kill humans. Thank goodness they are not true. These bumbling hunters look and sound a lot more fierce than they really are. The devils' bad reputation is largely undeserved.

You've probably seen Taz,™ the cartoon character. His behavior is based on that of real devils, although a lot of it is exaggerated. His never-ending appetite is funny—but it's one thing that isn't exaggerated. Devils are so food oriented that they were given the scientific name *Sarcophilus,* which means "meat lover."

Another thing about devils that is not exaggerated in the cartoons is their bad temper. They really are as mean as people think they are. Calling a devil grumpy would be too kind. They go far beyond grumpy. All Tassie devils are naturally ill-tempered and aggressive. Some, like cartoon Taz,™ fly into violent rages for no apparent reason. But some captive devils are dependable enough to be handled and

Cartoon Taz™ and a real-life devil show the fierceness that has made them both legendary.

petted by a careful keeper—a *very* careful keeper.

Devils are not big enough to be a real threat to humans. The weight of an average female is only 12 pounds. Even full-grown males rarely weigh more than 20 pounds.

Small as they are, devils are the biggest meat-eating mammal in their homeland. Like most Australian mammals, Tasmanian devils are marsupials. They have a pouch, like kangaroos or koalas. The earth's 4,000 mammal species are divided into three groups according to their reproductive plans: monotremes (MAHN-oh-treemz), which lay eggs; marsupials (mahr-SUPE-ee-ulz), animals that usually have a pouch in which they carry their babies, which are born only partially developed; and eutherians (you-THEER-ee-unz), like us, whose young are well developed at birth.

Australia is the only place that has all three kinds of native mammals. The island continent has the only two monotremes (echidnas and duckbilled platypuses); only two kinds of eutherians (rats and bats); but more than two-thirds of the world's 260 species of marsupials.

Marsupials are not restricted to Australia and nearby islands. About 70 species are native to the Americas. Only one, the Virginia opossum, can tolerate the cold weather of North America.

Many marsupials don't look very different from other mammals. But looks can fool you. They *are* different in some minor ways and in three major ones.

1. REPRODUCTION   The marsupials get their name from the Latin word *marsupium*, which means "pouch." Devils have pouches, but not all the marsupials do. Despite the group's name, it is not the pouch that sets them apart, but their *method* of reproduction. Marsupials have a single lower body opening, called a cloaca (kloh-AH-kah). It is used for waste disposal, for mating, and as a birth canal. All marsupials have a short gestation (time babies grow inside the mother's body) and give birth to tiny, partially formed young that

finish developing outside the mother's body. Although the eutherian method of reproduction is different from marsupials', it is not necessarily "better." Biologists think the marsupial method is just as successful.

2. BRAIN   A marsupial's brain is only half as large as that of a eutherian mammal the same size. Because the parts of the brain that store and process information are not well developed, marsupials, like monotremes, have a hard time adapting to unfamiliar situations. In this difference, they are inferior to the more intelligent eutherians.

3. ENERGY   Devils and all the other carnivorous marsupials are experts at conserving energy. Devils can, instantly and at will, cut their energy use in half. To do it, they go into torpor, a state that is similar to hibernation. Their body temperature drops from 100° F to 88° F, and their breathing rate and pulse are cut so dras-

Sleep or torpor? Devils love to lie in the sun, but it's hard to tell whether they are asleep or in an energy-conserving torpor.

15

tically that devils in torpor lie in a death-like trance. But unlike a hibernating animal, devils can zip between activity and torpor and back again in a matter of seconds. They are about the best in the animal kingdom at mobilizing energy in a hurry.

Devils don't look much like their closest relatives. Most of the meat-eating marsupials are small and mouselike. Devils—with their chubby bodies, short, stumpy legs, and massive, bone-crushing jaws—are definitely not mouselike. Their distinctive black and white coloring sets them apart from the other meat-eating marsupials too. It is easy to identify a devil by its markings. A few are solid black, but most have a white band across the chest and one around the base of the tail. Some have white spots on the body too.

The image of devils as great hunters is shattered when you see them run. They are slow and clumsy, with hindquarters so weak that they appear crippled. The forelegs, with their five-toed feet, have lots of power; but all the four-toed hind limbs can manage is a clumsy hop. The rocking, lurching movement of a galloping devil is so unusual that it cannot be mistaken for any other animal.

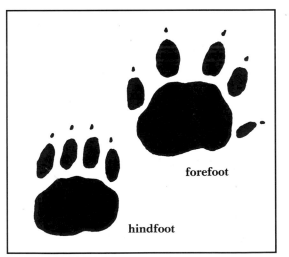

Knobby soles give devils good traction. Long claws help them dig. Young devils can even climb trees.

forefoot

hindfoot

Sack 3 Time

This may sound odd, but Tasmanian devils, like all marsupials, are born twice.

FIRST BIRTH (takes place in April–May, the beginning of Tasmanian winter, after a three-week gestation period)

A person would have to be very lucky to witness the "first birth" of a devil. The whole process takes less than five minutes and is practically ignored by the mother, who is 20,000 times bigger than the tiny babies that wriggle from her cloaca.

Blind, deaf, hairless, and small as a grain of rice (¼ inch), the babies are only partly formed. But ready or not, the little devils must now begin a race. The race course is only three inches long—the distance from the birth canal to the pouch—but it is the most important journey a devil will ever make. A devil female has four nipples inside her pouch and produces as many as fifty babies at a time. The only winners in the race for life are the four that find a nipple. Once they begin to suck, the mother's nipples enlarge, completely filling the babies' mouths, and they remain attached for 100 days.

For a long time, scientists thought that marsupial mothers helped their young into the pouch. But observations have shown that these specks of life reach the nipples under their own power. Using the sharp claws of their forepaws, the tiny racers climb up the mother's fur. The half-

Development of Devils in the Pouch

Drawings represent actual life size.

newborn
¼ inch long (sizes do not include tail)
¹⁄₂₀₀₀ of a pound
blind, deaf, hairless pink skin

4 weeks
½ inch long
eyes, lips, and ears begin to form

8 weeks
1 inch long
black skin but no fur
eyelashes and short whiskers can be seen

12 weeks
1½ inches long
fur, eyes open, ears erect, long whiskers
can make noise and open mouth

15 weeks
3 inches long
½ pound
fully developed

Janet Pedersen

formed rear legs dangle uselessly. No one understands how they find their way. It is probably smell that guides them; the blind, deaf racers have no other senses we know about.

During the first fifteen weeks the little devils are called pouch embryos. *Embryo* is a word usually reserved for unborn babies, but it describes the half-formed condition of marsupials in the pouch.

The pouch opening is controlled by a ring of muscles similar to our lips. The mother opens it several times each day, washes her babies, and removes waste products. But most of the time it is tightly closed, forcing the babies to breathe and rebreathe the same air. The level of carbon dioxide rises to 20 times that outside the pouch. This amount would suffocate an adult devil, but it doesn't seem to affect the babies.

The pouch keeps babies warm. They have no fur and cannot regulate their own temperature until the very end of the sack time. But it's too warm for fully furred devils whose temperature-control system

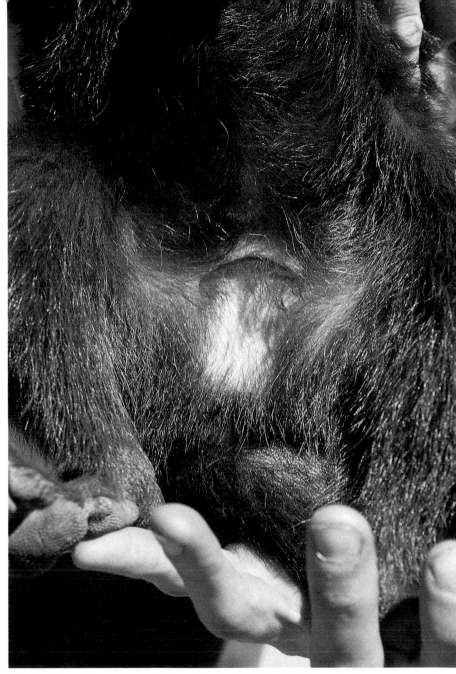

The devil's pouch opens toward the tail, and the babies climb in and out between the mother's hind legs. The male's pouch is similar to the female's, but only the female has nipples inside.

is operating. They overheat in the pouch, which is several degrees warmer than body temperature, and they move out. We know that temperature, not crowding, is the reason babies move to the nest, because a single baby leaves its relatively roomy pouch on the same day a litter of four does.

SECOND BIRTH (takes place in August–September, the beginning of spring)

Second birth is the day when devils leave the pouch. For fifteen weeks they live with their mother in a soft nest of leaves and grasses, reaching their heads into the pouch to suck milk several times a day. The nestlings are about the same size as a newborn kitten or puppy—three inches long and half a pound. At first, the mother leaves her babies in the nest when she goes hunting. Later they tag along, clinging with tooth and claw to the fur on her back. Every time she hits a bump, they tumble off. When they get bigger and stronger, the little devils run alongside her, hitching a ride only when they get tired.

Devils are good swimmers. They can't sweat, so they often get into the water to cool off. If a mother has babies in her pouch, she closes it tightly so they don't drown.

Seven months old and on their own. These littermates are on their first independent adventure. Their mother refused to let them into her pouch the morning this photograph was shot.

INDEPENDENCE (takes place in November–December, the middle of summer)

Now the one-pound youngster is ready to leave home. "Independence day" is in summer, so the devil has time to grow and build up enough fat reserves to make it through the cold Tasmanian winter. The time that mothers and nursing babies are together in the nest is the only time a devil lives with others of its kind.

Even baby devils fight. They use their littermates for practice in developing the skills they will need to survive on their own.

Their Own Worst Enemy

Baby devils have to be lucky devils to reach adulthood. Only one out of ten will grow to full size. Accidents and disease account for a few deaths, but the number-one killer of baby devils is other devils.

Devils are their own worst enemy. Unlike most animals, these mean little marsupials fight to the death with their own kind. The winner then eats the loser. Devils are cannibals!

Little devils do have a fighting chance, though. When they leave the pouch they are equipped with a full set of teeth. These are not temporary "baby teeth," but the 42 slashing, grinding, crushing weapons of an adult devil. The nestlings have only a brief time to practice using these teeth.

When they've been out of the pouch just three months, the mother devil stops feeding and guarding her young. Then they have to defend themselves "for real"— even against their own mother. She becomes an enemy, attacking and killing her own babies.

Any little devils that escape need two things in a hurry: protective cover and food. Hollow logs, rocky caves, or abandoned wombat holes are all good places to sleep. But the final selection of a nest depends on whether there is enough food nearby. Hunting territories average about two square miles. Devils do not protect this home range, even though they hate to share a meal. So, in places where there is plenty of food and shelter, such as Cradle Mountain, as many as thirty devils live and hunt in every square mile.

Devils try to get a share of all food discovered in their territory. Like sharks, they gather in a feeding frenzy at large carcasses. It is during the violence of these mass feedings that many young devils get killed.

Between animals of equal size, there is rarely physical combat. Devils test the strength of an opponent with a series of threats. Evenly matched opponents give each other every opportunity to retreat without being attacked. Most disputes are resolved through intimidating tooth displays, shoving and wrestling contests, and nerve-shattering screaming matches. Only if these threats fail do devils that are about the same size actually fight.

"Threats before fighting" is the rule, and all devils play by the rules. Once a safety mechanism to protect the species, the displays now threaten its survival. Animals that are not native to Tasmania, such as dogs and humans, don't play by devil rules. The devils seem to be unable to change the rules to protect themselves against these new predators that don't threaten before attacking.

Threats before a fight take many forms, including screaming, tooth clicking, foot stomping, and the release of smelly chemical weapons. Bright red ears are another sure sign that a Tassie devil is angry. A thick network of blood vessels just under the skin brings color to a devil's ears in much the same way our cheeks redden when we are angry or embarrassed.

In its most dramatic attempt to scare an enemy, the devil becomes a furry "tornado." Although the devil appears to be spinning in circles, it isn't. If you could slow the "tornado" down, you would see that the devil is actually alternating between two poses. First the devil gives its enemy a side view to make itself appear large and, therefore, strong. Then it switches to a front view, which shows off its dangerous-looking teeth. Devils change positions so quickly that it looks as if they are whirling around.

Red ears, erect whiskers, and a display of teeth show that this little devil is very angry.

When real fights like this one break out, they are very savage and often end in death.

Threats usually work. But if neither one backs off, they fight. Real combat is serious business. With ears laid back and eyes narrowed, the devils charge, their mouths wide open. In these head-on crashes, teeth are sometimes broken or knocked out.

If one of the devils realizes it is outmatched, it offers a cheek as a sign of submission. The dominant devil bites it— hard enough to draw blood. Most adult devils' faces are terribly deformed from the scars and scabs of these cheek bites.

Another way devils say "I quit" is by dropping spread-eagle on their bellies. At this point the weaker devil can still escape with nothing more serious than a bite on its retreating rump. Some arguments end with both devils backing off. It's not always clear which devil, if either, has won.

Devils' lives are short and violent. They are genuine tough guys, with what appears to be little concern for pain. Many of the devils we saw at Cradle Mountain were walking around with infected cuts, broken legs, dangling tails, lost toes, ripped-off ears, missing teeth, and other injuries. And those were the winners.

There are no losers left to walk around. Not when combat is to the death and beyond, to cannibalism.

By eating carrion (flesh of creatures that are already dead), devils help to control disease-carrying insects. Two devils can dispose of an entire kangaroo in about five minutes.

Devil's 5 Food

Tasmanian devils are not fussy eaters. They are sometimes called "garbage cans with teeth"—they gobble up almost any food that doesn't walk away. Devils happily munch rotten corpses that are crawling with worms or maggots. They have even been seen snacking on such strange items as rubber boots, shotgun shells, and flashlight batteries.

Meat is a devil's favorite food, though—meat in any size, shape, or degree of smelly decay. Devils are both predators and scavengers. The combination of these two food-gathering methods and a willingness to eat things most other creatures wouldn't dream of consuming gets devils all the food they need.

If big sources of meat are not available, devils will eat grubs or gobble up caterpillars and beetles. In summer they hunt for frogs, lizards, and the eggs and chicks of ground-nesting birds. When fruits and seeds are ripe, the greedy devils feast on them too.

What a devil eats depends on what is available. A coastal devil might grab a crab; suburban devils add humans' garbage to their nightly menu.

The variety of devil's food is awesome, and so is the quantity they eat. Devils can consume five, ten, even fifteen times their body weight in a single meal. One account tells of a devil that escaped from a zoo on mainland Australia. It was loose for only two nights, but during that time it ate 54 chickens, 6 geese, 1 sea gull, and a cat.

Tassie devils often camp out near a large carcass until all the meat is gone. A ranger reported that when two devils found a dead cow, they made a temporary home in its rib cage while they devoured the carcass. In two days they ate the entire cow— 60 times their body weight. Into these two black-and-white eating machines had gone not only all the meat, but all the bones, the hair, the skin, even the teeth.

Most of the killings once blamed on devils were probably done by the tree-climbing marsupial cat (quoll) or the marsupial wolf (thylacine, now probably extinct). But devils can and do kill, especially if they find trapped or small animals. An unguarded henhouse quickly becomes an empty henhouse in devil country. Devils in cartoons never catch Bugs Bunny; but in real life, Tasmanian devils often kill

Devils use their paws to position food or shove it into their mouths.

"Deviled eggs." Tasmanian devils put whole eggs into their mouths and pierce them with their sharp teeth. Then they suck out the contents and spit the shells out onto the ground.

and eat rabbits. However, it is as scavengers that they get most of their food.

While we were on location, Tara and I became scavengers ourselves. Armed with rubber gloves and big plastic bags, we drove up and down the highway near Cradle Mountain, looking for road kills to use as photography bait. We felt like ghouls as we scooped up dead kangaroos and possums. As the car filled up, the smells from our bait bags grew quite strong. A snake corpse wiggling with worms made me gag, but Side Spot did not find the snake disgusting at all. When we put it out as bait, he gobbled it up without a moment's hesitation and looked around for more.

Devils seem to thrive on food that can sting, bite, or even poison other animals. Their amazing digestive system is resistant to the disease-causing bacteria found in rotten meat, and it's tough enough to handle the devils' weird diet, including the porcupinelike echidna, which it swallows, spines and all. One fifteen-pound daredevil ate enough 1080 rat poison to kill forty people . . . and it didn't even get sick.

MEALTIME MANNERS FOR DEVILS

EAT AS MUCH AS POSSIBLE AS QUICKLY AS POSSIBLE. (Other devils may come and steal your food.)

DO NOT CHEW YOUR FOOD. (Devil teeth, adapted for tearing and crushing, are not useful for chewing.)

USE BOTH PAWS TO STUFF THINGS DOWN YOUR THROAT. (Be sure bones and other sharp objects are pointing the right way so they don't poke holes in your throat. Once they're in your stomach, don't worry. They will dissolve.)

ALWAYS SCREAM WITH A MOUTHFUL OF FOOD. (Who knows, it might frighten off hungry neighbors.)

DO NOT SHARE FOOD. (Hide your food; fling your body on top of it to protect it from others. Better yet, just steal it.)

PICK FIGHTS WITH SMALLER DEVILS. KILL AND EAT THEM IF YOU CAN. (It will get rid of some of the competition and get more food for you.)

Lords of Darkness

Devils prefer to live in a world of darkness. They are equipped for survival as either day or night dwellers, and they *choose* the night. This choice is not an unusual one. Day-active animals like us are vastly outnumbered by creatures of the night. Many of them could survive just as well in the daylight.

Most marsupials are nocturnal. Nearly 90 percent of them learned to deal with the hot, dry climate of their Australian homeland by limiting activities to the relatively cool nights. But, over a long period of time, the climate of Australia changed. Tasmania, for instance, is a cold, wet place now. But devils, which have the necessary skills to survive by day or night, have kept their nocturnal habits. They are the lords of darkness, as comfortable and successful in their world as we are in ours. The night holds few secrets from them.

Most animals that are active at night rely on smell to gather information. Tasmanian devils are no exception. The biggest part of their brain is that associated with the sense of smell. Human beings have made smelling machines such as smoke alarms and gas detectors, but none are able to sort out the chemical messages called scent as well as the devil's nose can. With its sensitive sniffer, a devil can find food by smell alone. Tracking smells is easier at night because odor particles are not carried up and away from the source, as they are in

The scary red glow in a devil's eyes is caused by light reflecting from the tapetum, a membrane that allows them to see a lot in dim light. But the "picture" they see is a blury black-and-white image.

the hot air currents that rise in the day.

To find food, the devil uses a regular search pattern, following trails that it has marked with its own scent. Marked trails are like odor maps that guide a devil through its home range. The smell messages also let other devils know the territory is occupied.

The marking substances, made in three special glands, are held until they are needed. They are stored in sacs located in the mouth, on the chest, and below the tail. Each releases a different smell or combination of smells. The meanings of many of these chemical messages are unknown to us. However, in the case of a nasty-smelling scent released only when a devil is upset, the meaning is clear enough: The "stinker" is angry!

When devils meet, they immediately begin to release odorous body chemicals, rubbing them on themselves, dribbling them on nearby objects, even spraying them on other devils that come close enough.

Devils lick their cupped paws and rub their own scented spit over their heads and necks. Mother devils use their stinky saliva to mark babies for the first few months, when the scent glands of baby devils are undeveloped. Babies marked with their mother's spit are safe from attack when they approach her in the dark.

From the way devils react to scent marking, it is obvious that some smells can contain threats. It would be interesting to know exactly what devils are saying when they spit their chemical insults at each other.

Sound, like smell, can penetrate the darkness, making it another good way to gather information at night. Tara learned firsthand that devils have excellent hearing. While she was taking photos of a group of devils quarreling over a dead kangaroo, she sneezed. Her sneeze, quiet compared to the screaming of the food frenzy, instantly attracted the attention of the devils. It must have sounded like the sneezing sound devils make before attacking, because the biggest devil rushed toward her. Apparently he thought Tara was going to attack him—and she certainly thought he was going to attack her! They stood three feet apart, screaming at each other. A scary few minutes passed before the devil retreated to munch kangaroo once more.

Devils are the noisiest of the marsupials. Their screams can be heard miles away. And the ten different devil calls that have been identified give them the biggest marsupial "vocabulary." Devil sounds include a few nonvocal messages as well. These include foot stomping, lip licking, and teeth clicking, all aggressive signals. The vocal calls are aggressive, too, with the exception of the distress call of the young. Sneezes and huffs signal attacks. A doglike bark establishes dominance after combat, and a particularly nasty growl does double duty as a threat and as a love call.

For a nocturnal animal, the devil relies on its eyes a lot. Many devil-to-devil messages are visual ones, probably because a devil's eyes are truly dual purpose, functioning well by day and equally well when there is one-millionth the amount of light.

Two adaptations give the devils their good night vision: a high percentage of the light-sensitive cells called rods, which detect motion in low light, and the tapetum (tah-PEE-tum), a special membrane behind the eye. It reflects light back into the eye, where it has a second chance to strike the rods.

In the dark, touch is an important sense. Some hairs on a devil's face have been modified into touch-sensitive organs. The scientific name for these long hairs is vibrissae, but most people call them whiskers. Each devil's whiskers are arranged in a unique pattern, like the lines of a person's fingerprint.

All these adaptations show how the devil has been "customized" by nature for its role as a night prowler.

Six hundred years ago, devils roamed the night all across the Australian mainland. Now they are found only on the island of Tasmania. Devils are a protected species, but there are mysterious fluctuations in the population. In 1976 the number of devils dropped so low that even

sightings of tracks were rare. A serious disease was suspected but never identified. By 1982 devils seemed to be on a comeback trail, but in 1990 the numbers began to drop again.

Tasmania's big meat-eating marsupial, the thylacine, also suffered from mysterious population fluctuations. It was given protected status too late. It is believed that the last wild marsupial wolf was killed in 1930. We can never bring the thylacine back, but we can lay aside sanctuaries, such as Cradle Mountain, to ensure that no more species will become extinct through our actions. Even the commonest of animals have disappeared from large portions of their former ranges.

Today, the Tassie devil lives only on the island of Tasmania. But because many Australians had the courage to protect one of nature's "unhuggables," the devil is still out there—screaming in the night.

Devil Facts

Common Name: Tasmanian devil
No special names for males, females, or babies. No special name for groups.

Scientific Name: Sarcophilus harrisii (sometimes listed as *Sarcophilus ursinus*)

Size: Adult male: average height at shoulder 12 inches; average length of body, 2 feet plus a 1-foot tail. Weight range: 12–25 pounds. Adult females about 15 percent smaller than males.

Color: Black, usually with white chest band and small white patches on the shoulders and above the tail. Occasionally albino (solid white) or all black.

Behavior: Nocturnal. Solitary. Savage.

Habitat/Range: Tasmania (an island off the south coast of Australia). Wide variety of habitats including forest, meadow, seashore, and around human settlements.

Food: Primarily meat, including carrion. Diet also includes insects, fruits, seeds, eggs, and garbage.

Life Span: Six years in captivity. Unknown in wild.

Gestation: Three weeks. Up to four young suckle in pouch for fifteen weeks, then live in nest and nurse another fifteen weeks.

Predators: Humans.

Population: Actual numbers unknown. Common in some areas.

Index